Small Business Sales How-to
Book #4

HOW TO DELIVER PROFESSIONAL SALES PRESENTATIONS & DEMONSTRATIONS

Pre-commitment agreement, focusing proof, closing, dealing with objections

Michael McGaulley

Published by Champlain House Media

www.Sales-Training-Source.com

ISBN: 9781386547358

ASIN: B07NVTC55T

Mera 3-11

For more information on the other books and guides in the Small Business Sales How-to Series:
http://salestrainingsource.com/

Contents

INTRODUCTION

Starting point: sales presentations and sales demonstrations are proof sources. That is, when planning a presentation or demonstration, it's crucial to keep in mind that the purpose is to prove something. What it is you are setting out to prove to the prospect depends on the situation.

Which means there should be no such thing as a "standard" or "canned" demonstration or presentation: each should be tailored to the specifics of this prospect and this potential sale.

What IS a "proof source?" Basically, a proof source can be anything that's needed to help you prove any part of the case you made to the Prospect.

That is, you may need to prove to the Prospect's satisfaction that your product or service can,

- fill the needs that you have uncovered in your earlier sales meeting with the Prospect; or can,

- do so within the cost you have claimed; or,

- do the job more efficiently or economically; or,

- do it better than a competing product; or,

- do it better than the existing method, whatever that may be; or,

- or . . . or . . . or any of a variety of things.

Precisely what it is that you need to prove — as well as the best kind of proof source to use — depends on what came up in the course of your discussions with the Prospect and others.

That may seem obvious enough: you match the proof source to what needs to be proven, and that what needs to be proven flows from what the Prospect is looking for.

It is obvious, of course. Regardless, salesperson give demonstrations and presentations for no real purpose other than for the sake of giving them. Why? Maybe because . . .

- they want to have something to fill in on this week's appointment book so they look busy; or,

- they want to get the feeling (or show the boss) the sense of progress being made; or,

- their (incompetent?) sales manager has set a quota on how many demos and presentations they are to give each month; or,

- it seems like a good idea; or,

- the prospect seems willing to sit still for a demo.

A skilled salesperson offers a demo or presentation for one reason only: to prove that this product or service can and will fill the specific need that this specific prospect has, and that it will fill that need better and more cost-effectively than other alternatives.

Quick review: why Prospects buy

If you have read my other books in this *Small Business Sales How-to Series—*

- **25 Sales How-to Tutorials:** A step-by-step guide primarily directed to new entrepreneurs, self-employed, and career changers.

- **Selling 101: Consultative Selling Skills.**

- *Sales Training Workshop Leader Guide* – an instructor guide for using *Selling 101* in class or sales team meetings.

— then you will likely recall the point I stressed: individuals and organizations, and the Prospects within organizations, buy if and only if they arrive at solidly Yes! answers to four fundamental questions.

That is, prospects, as they meet with you, hold four questions in mind:

- Do we face a **need**?

- Is that need **significant enough** to justify our spending some money to fill it?

- Will this product or service actually **fill that need**?

- Will it **fill the need better** or more cost-effectively than other approaches?

Those four questions provide the framework making the sale: as a salesperson, your objective should be to help them see that yes is the correct answer for them in that situation.

But what if you look at the situation and realize that the honest to-goodness correct answer is not Yes? An ethical, professional salesperson will so advise the prospect that this product is not right for him at this time. You may lose this sale, but will gain credibility for the future, or with referrals made by this Prospect.

But, assuming the answer is yes to each, these four questions then provide you the framework for making the sale.

If the Prospect tells you precisely what she needs to see proven, fine. That sets your direction.

But if the Prospect can't spell out, or isn't forthcoming on, what he needs to see proven, then these four questions, turned around, suggest the corresponding areas which may require more proof. Thus you may need to answer and prove that you have sound answers to those questions, that . . .

- there is a need, and,

- the need is significant enough to justify spending money to fill it, and,

- what you are offering will fill that need (or needs), and,

- will fill the need better and more cost-effectively than any other approach, either within the organization or through your competitors.

But there is usually another point that may also need to be proven before the sale can be made, and this is often unspoken: that you and your organization are reliable, experienced, professional, trust-worthy, and likely to remain in business at least long enough to fulfill your obligations under this sale.

To ascertain which of these (or other matters) are at issue, talk with the Prospect, ask questions, listen well, attending to both the spoken and unspoken concerns to isolate what is still at issue and needing proof.

Then select a proof source that can effectively back up your case. Among the more generally-helpful sources of proof are these:

- Samples of your work, or of the output produced by your product or service.

- Demonstrations of your product (or yourself) in action.

- Case studies of successful projects and references from satisfied customers, most often evidencing your reliability.

- Written proposals, most often to document costs or cost savings, or to put in writing assurances about timing, warranty, and the like.

In this book, we'll be focusing on the when-to and how-to of the most common proof sources — sales demonstrations and presentations.

Why it is a good use of your time to personally "present" something like a written proposal

A proposal is a kind of proof source: you use a proposal generally to document what will be done, within what time-frame, and at what cost.

You might feel that since a written proposal lays it all out in writing that there is no real need to "present" it personally. That is usually wrong.

Yes, you could mail (or fax or e-mail) that proposal or other documentation. That would save you time, both travel time and time on-site. After all, time is money, and you don't want to waste time, of course.

But saving that time may be short-sighted. Your overall objective is not to save time, but to make sales, and you may be wasting a significant selling opportunity if you merely mail that proposal . . . or if you simply drop it off at the Prospect's office and hope it will work its magic.

If you just mail it or fax it, or drop it off, chances are that it will get pushed to the bottom of the pile, and nothing will happen.

By personally "presenting" your proposal, work sample, or other kind of proof source, you ensure that the Prospect attends to it on a guaranteed date, while it is still relevant.

For one thing, you'll generally get a speedier response. Further, by retaining control, you ensure that you WILL get a response — it won't just get buried under other mail.

Even more importantly, by "presenting" the proposal or formal presentation, you gain the opportunity,

- to test the atmosphere during your presentation— how it is being received, who is pro, who con, and why.

- to gain valuable feedback, which may be useful both on this sale and in future sales.

- to clear up any difficulties or misunderstandings; and, if necessary,,

- to negotiate any final issues that stand in the way of the sale.

Bottom line: a presentation or demo is a key selling opportunity

A "presentation," in the sense we're using the word here, means a great deal more than merely walking in and handing the proposal to the Prospect.

We're speaking here in the broader meaning of presentation, which may mean a formal presentation (perhaps complete with PowerPoint, handouts, and all the rest), or may mean just delivering, and talking through, a simple cost proposal.

Your presentation is a key selling opportunity, as it gives you the chance to summarize the core messages of your proposal, and to respond to any concerns expressed by for the Prospect (that may be an individual or team who has Authority to buy, Need, and Dollars or budget), as well as any key Decision Influencers.

In short, a presentation or demonstration is your chance to prove your key points to the prospect . . . to prove that the answer to those five questions is yes, and that yours is the best way.

Part one: EARLY PREPARATIONS

To put this in context: In most cases, you'll make one or more sales calls before you get to the point of needing to present proof — whether in the form of a demonstration, a formal presentation, a proposal, or perhaps a free or test trial offer.

Let's pick it up there: you have made one (or several) calls on a Prospect; the Prospect is interested, but hesitates because she is not convinced that your product or service can do the job, or can do it cost-effectively, or can do it better than the present method, or than a competing product.

The proof source that you choose will flow from just what the Prospect is looking for.

- Perhaps a demonstration of your product in action is appropriate so the Prospect can see that it does all you claim.

- Or suppose you're a consultant, and you've done a preliminary analysis of what's needed. Now the Prospect wants you to present your findings and proposed solution to that Prospect and a working team of others who will then decide whether to engage your services to fix the problems you have uncovered.

We will be focusing here mainly on demonstrations and formal presentations, as you can easily adapt the framework to other types of proof.

To clarify: the demonstration or presentation may take place on the Prospect's premises, or in your office, or even in a third location, such as a rented conference room. The differences are mainly in the logistics involved, which we will be looking at shortly.

We begin with the idea of obtaining a "pre-commitment," which you would be wise to obtain before you agree to invest the time and effort of preparing a demo or presentation.

1. Crucial first step before developing any proof: Negotiate a "pre-commitment" with the Prospect.

You may offer at the end of your sales call on the Prospect to provide proof, such as a written proposal, a formal presentation, or a demonstration of the product in action.

Or, the Prospect may ask for proof — perhaps in so many words, or perhaps subtly, even sub-consciously or even non-verbally: if you are attentive, you may just "know" that this Prospect likes your product, but isn't quite convinced that it will do the job.

It's tempting to offer to provide any kind of proof source that would seem to do the job. It may be tempting, but usually is not wise . . . not until and unless the Prospect is willing to reciprocate by making an initial agreement in return for your investing time and effort in preparing that proof.

Before investing the time and resources in developing any kind of proof source, it is essential that you get a firm agreement from the key Prospect on four key issues:

1. The key people, especially the Prospect, will be personally present for your personal delivery of the agreed-upon proof.

2. *The Prospect will set aside a guaranteed block of time*, typically about 30-45 minutes at the most. That means that the Prospect will be present, and take no calls during that time.

3. *Precisely what is to be proven.* There is no point in your proving A if the Prospect's concern is whether the product can accomplish B. Nor is there any point in coming in to prove anything if the Prospect does not have a clear purpose in mind.

4. A pre-commitment that if you do prove certain agreed-upon points, the Prospect will be prepared at that point to sign an order. ("A pre-commitment" is more or less the equivalent of we might call a "handshake deal.")

You aren't going to get, nor should you ask for, a written agreement on these four points. But the Prospect should be willing to make at least these commitments: to be personally present, for a clear block of time, with a clear objective.

If the Prospect is not willing to agree, then it is almost certainly not worth your time to proceed.

What if the prospect won't agree to the "Pre-commitment?"

By asking for these four commitments up front, you are asking a lot in advance from the Prospect. There is a risk that the Prospect may not agree to these conditions.

But suppose the Prospect won't pre-commit? What have you really lost? Most likely, not very much, at all. After all, it's a considerable investment of time and energy on your part to plan and make a presentation or set up a demonstration, or to write a proposal. If the prospect is not willing to meet these moderate pre-conditions at the start, does it really make sense for you to invest in the other work of setting up a presentation or other proof source on the mere hope that it may open up a sale?

In that case, you need to be realistic about the chances of making the sale. If the Prospect is unwilling to make that commitment, ask yourself if there is any real point in proceeding to gather and present the proof . . . at least until you have addressed the underlying reasons for his unwillingness to make that agreement.

Insisting on that pre-commitment is a subtle but effective way of ensuring that the person is serious about having you proceed, and of ensuring that they have the level of Authority, Need, and Dollars that they claim to have.

There's also the matter of "opportunity cost"—the time you spend on developing this proof for this prospect takes away from your ability to work with other potential clients. The Prospect can't reasonably expect you to make this investment of time and opportunity cost unless he is seriously interested, and ready to commit.

Probe to find why the Prospect is unwilling to commit

If the Prospect balks at this agreement, ask questions and explore why they hesitate. If it is something that you can deal with, do so.

But if you hear only a string of nebulous excuses, then it may be best to cut your losses and move on. Granted, if you pull the plug now, you will have wasted the effort invested to this point in the selling process. But if the Prospect is not willing to make these modest commitments, then the chances are very high that you will only waste more time and effort on a lost-cause, dead-end effort.

Other reasons why you should insist on the conditions

Some salespersons are reluctant to push for this kind of Pre-commitment, believing that it is better not to ask the customer for anything at all until they finally ask for the order. But that bears risks:

- For one thing, it projects low confidence in the value of your product or service. If it is good, you don't have to give it away.

- Besides, if you fail to get some commitment from the Prospect, then the risk is all on your side: you invest time, energy, and opportunity cost, while the Prospect invests nothing, not even to commit to be on-hand for the hour it would take for you to present your proof source.

- People tend to value that which costs: if all the cost is on your part, then the Prospect probably won't value the result as much as if he had to invest some of the cost, as well.

Bottom line: respect the value of your own time. Do not commit to preparing or presenting proof until you get a commitment from the Prospect in return.

2. *Get a specific appointment from the Prospect for the time for the presentation or demonstration.*

Earlier, as part of the pre-commitment you gained from the Prospect before starting the proposal, you got the Prospect to agree to set aside uninterrupted time for this presentation.

It may take you a few days or more to assembly the elements of the presentation or demonstration. When all is ready — or nearly so— phone back the Prospect to settle on a time for this appointment.

This may be a couple of days, or maybe a week or so, after your previous contact, so it is a good idea to *remind* the Prospect of that agreement, that he or she agreed:

1. To be personally involved — and physically present, not just through a subordinate — for the review of the proof you present, whether that is to be a demonstration, presentation of a proposal, or whatever else is agreed upon; and,

2. To set aside that block of time, agreeing to no interruptions; and,

3. That you and this Prospect had defined clearly, in advance, precisely what needs to be proven; and,

4. To agree to buy if you do prove these agreed-upon factors.

How long a time-block to ask for will vary. As a general rule, try to work within the range of 20 to 45 minutes, depending on the dollars involved and the complexity of the situation. In estimating the time you need, be sure to allow for questions and discussion.

When you call for the appointment, make clear from the start that you will need a block of uninterrupted time free from phone calls and other interruptions:

> *"This meeting should take about 30 minutes. I'd very much appreciate it if you can arrange to have your phone calls held for that time. Will that be possible?"*

Be ready in case the Prospect responds, "Oh, it's not necessary for us to meet. Just mail it to me, and I'll look it over and get back to you shortly."

Don't believe it. You have invested significant time and effort in preparing the proposal: make sure you get the benefit by personally presenting it. Even though the Prospect may have the best of intentions of reading it later, it never works out as planned: the fact of life is that other calls and crises always intervene.

However, getting into a "But you promised to be present" mode is counterproductive.

Instead, try to finesse it in a tactful way. For example, you might explain that there are "some options that you need to raise with the key people."

Or that "in the course of developing the proposal (or the survey on which the data was based) I came up with some broader recommendations beyond the scope of the proposal." (Obviously, promise only what you can deliver.)

Determining who else should be present

Before concluding the call, find out from the Prospect precisely who will be present at that meeting, whether it is a presentation or demonstration.

The Prospect herself — that is, the person (or group) with Authority, Need, and Dollars — MUST be present.

DO NOT give the presentation until this Prospect (or Prospect team) will commit to being present — even if that means waiting days or weeks for the presentation. (On this, keep in mind the sales rule: Many people can say no, but only the boss can say yes. If you present to those who can only say no, then you lose the opportunity.

Though the final choice of who to invite belongs to the Prospect, you can certainly suggest the names of the Decision Influencers who were helpful as you made your earlier calls. These would be people who gave you useful information, or showed you the present system and perhaps tipped you off on some existing flaws. Mention them by name, as "they contributed some extremely helpful ideas."

Here's a simple worksheet to work from:

Decision influencers and others you think should be present	Why each

Background: about Decision Influencers

"Decision Influencers" are people who, while they don't have the final Yes authority, still have significant input on how the actual Prospect calls it.

Precisely who the Decision Influencers are will vary with the organization and situation. They will usually include the heads of the departments that actually use your product, and perhaps some of the hands-on users of the product, as well.

Decision Influencers may also include key financial advisors, the firm's most experienced technical specialist in this area, or the Prospect's trusted secretary.

While Decision Influencers are usually below the Prospect on the organization chart, they may also be higher-level people, such as the Prospect's mentor.

3. "Touch base" in advance with any key Decision Influencers who will be attending.

The decision on who to invite belongs to the Prospect. You cannot invite them on your own initiative, but you can suggest the names of those who have been helpful and supportive . . . or who you may still need to win over.

Therefore, as your work on the proposal nears completion, it is a good idea to check back with these people, especially department heads and others who have been helpful, and briefly outline some of what you might term your "preliminary findings."

Do this both as a courtesy to them, and as a way of eliciting helpful early feedback. If they have concerns, you can incorporate their suggestions now, in advance of the meeting. That way, you can still amend or correct your approach, and not be caught off-guard in front of the Prospect.

A further advantage in bringing Decision Influencers in at this point: by consulting them and listening to their input, you give them a sense of shared ownership of the end-product, and they may be supportive allies as you make your presentation.

Again, the decision on whether to invite these Decision Influencers to the presentation belongs to the Prospect. You can discreetly sound out whether the influencers would be free to attend a meeting on certain dates, but do not overstep by inviting them on your own.

4. Plan and prepare the logistics of the meeting

Here's a starter checklist of the logistical issues to tend to. Add or delete items according to your individual situation. Note that the logistics will vary with whether you will be presenting at your site, or at the Prospect's location.

- Where will the demo or presentation be held? Is the room reserved for that time?

- Do you have any keys needed to gain access to that room?

- If necessary, has Security at the gate or reception area been notified that visitors will be arriving?

- Prepare any slide shows, or other audio-visuals. (See items 6-8 below for tips.)

- Will you be giving handouts? Do you know how many copies will be needed?

- If this will be held on your premises, will you have coffee or cold drinks to offer?

- If on your premises, are there other members of your team who should be introduced, such as your manager (if any), tech people, customer service staff, and the like?

5. *Plan and prepare your demo or presentation.*

Your proof source — whether a demonstration, presentation, proposal or whatever — typically follows an earlier face-to-face meeting with the Prospect, at which you discussed the Prospect's needs, and how your product can fill those needs.

What you discovered, or discussed with the Prospect or Decision Influencers in your earlier sales calls, will usually help form the framework for structuring the proof you provide.

We cover how to ferret out Prospects' needs, and how to express the capabilities of your product or service in the companion volume in this series, Sales Training Tutorials.

The template or worksheet in that book will give you a good start in organizing and structuring the information for your demo/presentation:

Need	Why/how it matters to this prospect	What it costs to leave that need unfilled	How I or my product / service can fill that need	How my product / service can help pay for itself by filling that need

Important point: here we refer to using these templates or worksheets in organizing your data and ideas. But these same formats — cleaned up and put onto flip-charts or presentation slides — will also serve as useful visual aids to use during the actual presentation.

Here is another template that may serve as a useful tool in structuring the information.

Need	How my product / service can help fill each of these needs	Value of filling those needs

6. In your preparation, focus on *KEY SELLING MESSAGES.*

When you're planning the presentation, decide what *truly crucial points* you want to make.

These are the "hot-buttons" to get the buyers excited, and the items you want them to leave remembering. Concentrate on those. It's far better to make a few core messages clearly than to spread too thin, sowing confusion.

But even as you prepare to speak of these hot-buttons, keep the larger objective in mind: a presentation or demonstration is a proof source.

That means that you don't just present all the good points; rather hit those hot-buttons in the context of what you are there to prove. If the objective is to prove that your product can meet cost targets, focus on that, and put the hot-buttons in that context.

If the objective is to prove that your product is more productive than a competitor's product, then prove that case.

If a hot-button—regardless of how "hot" it seems—does not relate to what your demo or presentation is to prove, then don't use it. It will only distract.

That is, you may not plan to use it, but still do hold that hot-button in reserve. It may just come in handy, after you've proven the main case, to call upon as a way of projecting a sense of additional value.

7. *As you prepare, VISUALIZE the scene and REHEARSE MENTALLY.*

That is, don't just throw some ideas into your head and expect to ad-lib the presentation.

Prepare to the level that you can TALK through the key messages in a normal, conversational manner — that is, so you are talking TO the people in the group, not talking AT them.

Don't memorize your talk (that comes across as stiff and boring), but you do need to go over it until you have a firm memory of your framework.

Your aim is to project that you are fully in control of your material. If you can't remember your key points without reading or looking at your notes, how can you expect the Prospect and Decision Influencers to remember what you have said?

Using Visualization

Beginning in the mid-1970's, many Olympic and professional athletes began making a practice of running though entire games or competitions in their minds, before they actually took place. They would visualize all elements, from getting ready, to the first moments, to a winning conclusion. (Some refer to this as "quiet time," others "visualization", or "a semi-meditative state".)

In a sense, they were mentally rehearsing what was to come. By working through in their minds, they prepared for the unexpected, and develop a sense of confidence. They also "programmed" their minds and movements.

I'm suggesting the same: don't memorize what you will say, but do run through — in a quiet zone, maybe a room, maybe just your mind — what you will say, how and where you will move, how you will project non-verbally, and how you will respond to questions and objections.

8. Prepare your visual aids and sales agreement

What visual aids should you use? Well, that depends . . . depends on what your product or service is, and what aspect you are proving.

That said, give thought to what kinds of visual aids can help you make your points, clearly and strongly. Those are,

- Flip-chart or a smaller A-frame desktop presentation aid. Or a tablet computer.

- If the situation and group size are appropriate, you could use your laptop and PowerPoint slides. That may be ideal if there are only a couple or three people present; for a group much larger, you may need a projector, and a screen, and on and on with cables and outlets.

- With smaller groups, such as three or four people sitting around a conference table, a simple notebook size A-frame may be ideal. Or use your laptop as a presentation aid.

- You could use a chalk-board or large pages on a presentation easel, but caution: unless you're very skilled, and a very good hand-printer, that may come across as unprofessional.

- In deciding whether to use overheads or other media, call the Prospect's secretary a few days ahead to find out how large the meeting room will be, and to get a final count of how many people will be present. Also check on electrical outlets or high-speed internet connections, if needed.

- If you use handouts or work samples, use them with caution: make them outline form only: otherwise, you'll find your audience reading the text, ignoring what you're saying.

Finally, kept out of sight until you need it, a sales order or sales contract, with customer information (name, address, etc.) already filled in.

Typical pages

If you're an old sales hand, feel free to skip this; I'm including it for "newbies".

Prepare separate pages for each item you will want to focus on. Here are some typical pages that you will likely include.

Cover page. This is a small professional touch, included to show that this demo or presentation was specially created for this Prospect. If you can get a copy of the Prospect firm's logo, that is even better. Some organizations will not let you have a copy of their logo — even though that same logo is on their letterheads or brochures. If that's the case, you might scan the logo and enlarge it.

A presentation to

**Research Branch
XYZ Corporation**

**by Robin Weston
GEM Manufacturing**

Date

Proposed objectives. Here put in writing the objectives that were agreed upon earlier, back when you obtained the Pre-commitment that the Prospect will buy if you can prove that your product or service will meet those agreed-upon objectives.

Objectives of this demo:

To show how the GEM 4500 can meet these agreed-upon needs of the XYZ Corporation:

☐   **Produce more than ___**

☐   **At a cost of less than ___**

☐   **With down-time of less than ___**

As you "prove" each of these points, pause to ask whether the Prospect agrees that this objective has been met. If yes, put a big check-mark in the check-box.

If the Prospect hesitates in agreeing, probe to find what is keeping them from agreeing, then deal with that concern.

Handouts, work samples, etc.

Here again it depends on precisely what it is you are selling, and what you need to prove.

A short history of your company may be relevant, if you need to prove that your firm has the experience and stability to do the job. If those are not at issue, then that could be just distracting clutter.

Samples of projects you have performed for other clients may be relevant. (But, caution, don't hand out samples of work that you have done for other clients without their clear permission.)

Another caution we'll be making later, but it bears repeating here: keep control of your handouts and samples. If you put them in a pile by the door, the attendees will pick them up as they come in, and will probably be reading instead of listening to what you are saying.

Partially-completed sales contract or equivalent

Be sure to have this ready before you begin the demo or presentation.

Both you and the prospect know that this contract is the focus of the demo, so there is no point in playing games with it. That means, you should have it at hand, partially-completed, ready to use.

"Partially-completed" means that you have already filled in the Prospect's name (or company name), address and basic information of that sort.

Why do this in advance? Why risk wasting an order blank? Because if you have to pause while you collect and fill in this basic information, the Prospect may begin to wonder about your professionalism — and your confidence in making the sale. ("He knew I was coming in for this demo, so why didn't he take the trouble to do this first?)

Normally do not fill in matters like quantity, price, and the like. If you leave those spaces open, you might be pleasantly surprised to find the order comes in for more than you had expected.

Depending on your situation and the customs of your industry, as an alternative to using the sales contract, you may be better to prepare an Action Plan, (sometimes called Implementation Plan), including the steps or phases you are to complete, along with a time line for doing so.

Again, depending on the situation, the Prospect's "signing off" on this Action Plan might be tantamount to signing a contract.

For more on how you can use this sales contract or proposed Action Plan as a tool for closing, see Tutorials 18 and 19 in my book, *Sales Training Tutorials.*

Information at www.SalesTrainingSource.com.

Part two: DELIVERING THE PRESENTATION OR DEMONSTRATION

Keep in mind WHY you use these proof sources, such as demonstrations, proposals, and formal presentations: To prove that what you are selling can meet needs that are of prime importance to the customer.

Your product (or service) may do many things, but probably only certain of those capabilities will really matter to this Prospect.

How do you determine which of those capabilities matter to this unique Prospect?

Basically, by asking questions, and by listening — listening both to what is said as you meet with the Prospect in your earlier sales calls, but listening also to what is unsaid . . . and "listening" also to the Prospect's non-verbal signals.

In short, if the Prospect agreed that certain needs are vital, then your demonstration should prove how your product can fill those needs, both effectively and cost-effectively. (You would lock in these objectives via the Pre-commitment we discussed in Part One, just above.)

A reminder: as proof sources, demonstrations are to DEMONSTRATE — that is, to show. Don't let your words get in the way. Let the product or work sample do most of the talking.

Where we are in the process

As we begin this next section. We assume that you have finished all the preliminaries detailed in Part One, and that the day of your demonstration (or presentation) is here.

Section A: Preliminaries

1. Arrive early to set up. Work through this checklist.

If it's taking place on your own premises, then you already know where the light switches and electrical outlets and coffee machines are.

But if you'll be working in the Prospect's office, or in borrowed space, then you need to settle things in advance.

Here's a quick starter checklist for when you're presenting on others' turf. Add to it from your experience.

- Are you legally parked? (It could mess up a great presentation if you are told you have five minutes to move your car before it is towed.)

- Is it clear to the Prospect's secretary that you are here for a scheduled appointment with the Prospect and others? (It could be that a temp is filling in, and hasn't thought to check the calendar.)

- Has the Prospect's secretary alerted the attendees on the list that you are on-site and will be ready to go at the time scheduled?

- Are you sure you have all your stuff—like laptop, A-frame or flip-chart, handouts, samples, extension cord, extra business cards?

- Are enough chairs already in place for the attendees you expect?

- You might ask the secretary if the Prospect has arranged to have calls held. (It's not your place to demand this, but a gentle reminder to an assistant can work wonders.)

- Other way around: have you turned off your own cell-phone and any other electronic toys that might go "Beep!"

- Do you have paper and pen out and ready to make notes of unexpected points raised, or of follow-up you may be asked to provide?

2. "Own" your block of time.

You have invested your time and expertise in addressing a problem on behalf of this organization.

You are now here to present a solution to a real need, one that was recognized as significant by the Prospect at your earlier meeting.

You obtained the Prospect's "Pre-commitment" to set aside this time, in exchange for your investment of effort.

This block of time, therefore, BELONGS to you. Therefore, ACT LIKE YOU OWN IT, not as if the Prospect and others are doing you a favor by listening.

The first step to "owning" your time comes as your arrive for the presentation: remind the Prospect that you and she have agreed on a set time (whatever that was: 30 or 45 minutes). If the Prospect doesn't immediately direct all calls to be held during that time, you might gently remind, saying something like, "Will you want to have your calls held?"

Second step to owning your time: Control the copies of the proposal, as well as any handouts, samples, and the like.

- Hand out the written proposal only after you have talked through the overview and other key points. Otherwise, if you give it out too early, you'll find yourself talking to a sea of scalps as the attendees focus on reading the handouts, ignoring what you're saying.

- Control the group's attention focus, so that they all attend to your central messages at the same time.

- Keep the copies of the proposal or handouts in your briefcase, out of sight until you are ready for them.

Pass the handouts only when the time is right for you. Otherwise, you will be talking to the tops of readers' heads, and the Prospect will wonder why you got everyone together to do a group reading.

Third step to owning your time: project, via your body-language, confidence and mastery of the subject. (For tips on projecting and reading non-verbals, see Part Three of this book.)

Section B: Working through the Six Key Phases

Here we assume that you have finished all the preliminaries, and that the day of your demonstration (or presentation) is here.

Demos and formal presentations are much alike in many ways, so what we say here applies to both.

The key difference is that in a demo you are demonstrating how something works or looks, while in a presentation you are typically leading the group through a proposal or other documentation, such as a report or study results.

Once the Prospect and her team of Decision Influencers are in place, you have six key phases to work through. (You might think of these six as "gates" to go through, rather than as a rigid series of steps. Be flexible: sometimes you may be able to combine the functions of a couple of the gates into one.)

Here's overview of those six key phases. We'll be looking at the how-to of each in the pages following.

1. Set the context with an Opening Benefits Statement.

2. State and confirm agreement on these objectives. Check for completeness. If appropriate, add any others suggested by the Prospect.

3. Confirm the Pre-Commitment you obtained earlier.

4. Conduct the body of the demonstration.

5. Deal with questions, comments, and objections.

6. Close with a close.

1. Set the context with an Opening Benefits Statement.

A "Benefits Statement" is a brief, "netted-out" summary of what you intend to prove, and of what it ultimately DOES FOR the organization.

The principal purpose of the Opening Benefits Statement is to gain the Prospect's attention at the start of the demo or presentation.

The OBS should be brief, and should summarize some ways in which you will be able to help.

A model Opening Benefits Statement follows. Note how it's direct, and to-the-point.

Note also how it speaks in terms of what the product DOES FOR the client, not of what it IS, nor of technical details.

> *"I'm here today to demonstrate the GEM 4500 . . . and more specifically to show how it can increase your unit's productivity in turning out the monthly ABC report, as well as in balancing the weekly output totals. These were, as you recall, the key needs we turned up in our earlier meeting."*

1. Confirm agreement.

Confirm agreement on the objectives that you and the Prospect worked out earlier for this presentation or demonstration. Check for completeness. If appropriate, add any others suggested by the Prospect. Here's a model you can adapt to fit your situation:

> *"On the basis of our earlier discussion, I believe that these are the three major objectives of greatest importance to you. First . . ."*

Whenever possible, print these agreed-upon objectives in advance on a flip- chart or other visual aid. That done, you can point to them to buttress your words.

Then ask of the group, "Are there any others that should be added?" If there are, print them on the visual so you can tick them off as you cover each point.

Generally, any additional objectives suggested by the group will be refinements of ones earlier agreed upon, or at least objectives you can adapt to.

If new objectives are raised now

Supposedly, the objectives were detailed in the earlier Pre-commitment. Notwithstanding, the Prospect or other person may suggest other objectives to be covered in this session. They may be easy to deal with, or not, so listen carefully as any additional objectives are suggested.

Very likely, these new objectives will be easy enough to cover with your existing preparation, handouts, and samples.

But may not want to commit to something new that you have not prepared for, or that is outside the scope of your demonstration. If that happens, be direct:

"That's raising a wholly-new issue, beyond what we had earlier agreed upon as essential to be covered in today's product demonstration."

The Prospect may intervene on your behalf, saying in effect that this suggested new issue is not significant enough to impact today's presentation, or to slow down the prospect of the sale.

But what if it's the Prospect herself who raises that new objective, or determines that it is important, after all? You could stand on your rights under the pre-commitment. But there are obvious risks to that approach.

A better approach is to pause at that point and treat the proposed new objective as you would respond to it if it were an objection.

For how to respond to objections and questions, see the companion book in this *Small Business Sales How-to Series*: **Sales Training Tutorials**, particularly Tutorials 20-23. That suggests a five-phase model approach. Here's a quick overview:

1. Explore.

2. "Listen through" to this Prospect's response.

3. Restate, if appropriate.

4. Respond to what they actually said.

5. Move on without getting bogged down.

Information on **Sales Training Tutorials** and my books in the Small Business How-to Series:

www.SellingFaceToFace.com

As you EXPLORE, begin by finding out why that new objective suddenly seems important to the Prospect.

Perhaps you can show how the same end can be accomplished in other ways through your product.

If it's not something you can easily deal with, PROBE to find how important it really is. You may well find that it's only an afterthought or a "nice-to-have," not a "must-have."

You may be able to point that out to the group. Indeed, your questions may well defuse the issue: as you probe to find how important it is, the issue may deflate itself.

In any case, deal with that issue, then move on. If you can resolve it, say so. If you can not resolve it, be up-front and say that, too. Then get the demo back on track showing how your product does fill the agreed-upon objectives.

Don't let yourself get bogged down on this or any other question, objection, or side issue. Deal with it, then move on.

Additional benefits of confirming the initial objectives, and asking if there are other objectives

- It brings you and the Prospect into initial agreement, setting the tone for further agreements to come.

- It helps you focus your demonstration in areas that are in fact significant to this Prospect, and the team-members who may be present. There is no better way to find what is important than to ask.

- It breaks the ice and sets up a dialogue at the start in a way that gets the Prospect team actively involved. This helps break down any barriers that may exist. As a result, the Prospect will tend to be more open, less defensive. Having spoken once, she will be more likely to do so again . . . thereby giving you valuable continuing feedback.

- Finally, giving the Prospect the chance to add or change items on the list of objectives helps overcome any feelings he may have of being coerced or manipulated.

Application exercise

Develop at least three different Pre-commitment questions. Be sure to write them down, as a memory aid, not a memorized script. Rehearse them until they feel comfortable, and you can ask them smoothly and with assurance. Feel free to model on the examples above.

1.
2.
3.

3. Confirm the Pre-commitment you and the Prospect made earlier.

After you have gained agreement on the objectives that are to be accomplished via this presentation or demonstration, then move on to confirm the Pre-Commitment that you obtained earlier from the Prospect. Here's a model:

> *"We agreed earlier that if I can prove to your satisfaction how the GEM 4500 can meet these objectives, you'll be prepared to order it now for your use. Are we still in accord?"*

The Prospect's answer will normally be yes, since you already obtained this commitment before scheduling this demo.

But if the answer is No, explore why before proceeding. Find what is holding back a decision, and deal with it.

However, as always in dealing with objections or hesitations, don't let yourself get bogged down. If you get back on track and move on, chances are that these minor concerns will be forgotten. But if you let them take over, the sale will be lost.

In other words, since you have come this far to make the presentation or the demonstration, you might as well proceed to give it, even if the Prospect seems to want to renege on the pre-commitment.

What if the Prospect is unwilling to confirm the earlier pre-commitment?

Gaining a pre-commitment naturally follows agreement on the objectives. That is, once you have specified the objectives that are appropriate (and the Prospect has agreed that these are indeed appropriate), then it is logical to ask,

"If I can show you how [my product or service] can meet these objectives will you be prepared to commit to what I have recommended?"

This pre-commitment is simply to make sure that you and the Prospect are in tune, not an attempt to force a decision before you have demonstrated your proof.

Again, if the Prospect is reluctant to make this pre-commitment at this time, the explore what holds her back. Among the reasons may be these:

- Some hidden objectives exist which you failed to bring up, and which are crucial to this Prospect or organization.

- You sought this pre-commitment too soon, before the Prospect felt comfortable. If so, simply continue with the demo or presentation.

- This individual may not be the real or the only decision maker. Ideally, you should have found this out much earlier, but some Prospects are reluctant to admit that they don't hold all the power they would like.

In dealing with this situation, the ideal approach would be to pause while the others needed for the decision are brought in. In the real world, this is usually not practical, so it's best to finish this presentation or demo, and then ask this person to help you bring the proper decision maker to another sales presentation or demo. If you're lucky, they may simply need to "go upstairs" and recommend the purchase to the boss.

4. Conduct the body of the demonstration or presentation.

The objectives you negotiated earlier with the Prospect (as part of the earlier Pre-commitment) will normally serve as topic headings in structuring your coverage. That is,

- Resist the temptation to take the Prospect on a guided tour of every aspect and capability of your product.

- Instead, structure your coverage to show how each of the agreed-upon objectives can be accomplished.

As you finish your coverage of each objective, pause to confirm that they understand the points you have made, as well as why you made that point.

- Make sure they understand how this aspect of your product fills the specified need.

- If their understanding does not seem to be clear, or if they hesitate or disagree, pause to find their root concerns and deal with them before moving on to the next objective.

Take positive action to confirm that the Prospect understands each major point you make and also understands its value. You can gain that confirmation by asking questions like these:

- "Can you see where that would be useful in your operation?"

- "What other applications for this feature can you think of in your office?"

- "Is it clear why I demonstrated this feature?" (Use this kind of direct question to confirm if something in the Prospect's face or body language indicates she is confused or troubled.)

Don't be shy about making comparisons

You may feel it's bad form to "talk down" the competition. You may even feel it's best to pretend the competition doesn't exist.

That's usually a dangerous restraint. Most likely, the Prospect knows about the competition, and is wondering why and how your product or service is better. That's why it's usually best to be direct in comparing your proposed method and their present system (if one is in place):

> *"Presently, getting your monthly ABC Report out takes, by your estimate, an average of 170 working hours, and effectively stops all other work being done in the section for the final week of each month. When you install the GEM 4500, the same report will be produced with 25 clerical hours, plus 10 hours of management time — a tremendous saving in time."*

When you have the agreement of the Prospect and her team that you have proven your product's ability to meet each objective, check it off on your flip-chart, chalk-board, A-frame, or other visual aid (to make a clear signal that you have meet that standard), then move on to focus on the next objective.

Tip

Treat your product with extreme respect. Handle it with the loving care that you would a priceless family heirloom.

Treat your samples with equal reverence. If the samples are paper, handle the sheets as if they were fragile medieval parchments of incomparable value.

5. Deal with any questions, comments, and objections.

In dealing with objections and questions, use the approach we have covered earlier. The core is always **Explore, Listen Through, Restate, Respond Positively**. Then **Move On** without getting bogged down.

Very likely, some of the people who have worked with you (Decision Influencers) will make favorable comments. Don't let those positive comments slip away into the air. Pick up on them, support them, amplify them as appropriate, as in this model following. For example, a department head may say,

> *"This is what we've needed for a long time, to deal with that backlog in (whatever it is)."*

"You're absolutely right, Mr. Jones," you respond. "You and I talked about that need when we met. You pointed out how _____ "

Handling favorable comments

If the Prospect or any member of the team comments favorably, agree with that statement, and expand the appropriate benefit:

> *"You're right, Ms. Prospect, the GEM 4500 does have a very quick response time: that means less waiting, and, therefore, greater productivity for your people."*

Handling unfavorable comments

If the comment is unfavorable, or if it is a clear objection, draw on the five-phase method for responding to objections. For a quick overview, see the box in item 2, above. For a more detailed how-to, see Tutorials #20-23 in **25 Sales How-to Tutorials**, which is another in this

Small Business How-to series. Information at
www.SellingFaceToFace.com

Basically,

- Rephrase the comment or objection in question
  form:

*"If I understand your point, you're wondering
whether the GEM 4500 will be able to _____. Is that
a fair statement of your concern?"*

- If it is an easy-to-answer objection, answer it
  directly:

*"Yes, the GEM 4500 can do that, and does it well. Let
me briefly demonstrate that capability."*

- If it is difficult to answer, then minimize it, and
  stress other relevant benefits of the product:

*"No, the GEM 4500 doesn't have an oversize
capability, but from our discussion of your needs, the
sorting capability would be more often used, and is a
tremendously helpful feature to have when you're
preparing a last-minute job."*

Reminder: stay within your agreed-upon time frame

The Prospect gave you the time you asked for. Now you
need to fulfill your part of the bargain by finishing within
that allotted time.

But what if there are significant interruptions? Highly
likely, the Prospect will signal flexibility in giving extra
time to compensate for the minutes you lost.

If not, and if you really do need the time, ask the Prospect's permission to make up the time:

> *"I had structured this around the 30-minute period that we had agreed upon. It seems we lost about ten minutes to those interruptions. May I borrow back those ten minutes? If you agree, I will make a point of finishing within my overall estimate of a total 30-minutes. Is that agreeable?"*

6. *Close with a close.*

"Closing" by asking for what you want is the natural punctuation mark concluding your presentation.

You'll find that unless you DO conclude with a close the presentation will have an unfinished feeling. You'll generally sense the Prospect and others floundering, with a feeling of "Where do we go from here? What do we do now? What do you want from us?"

What to close for

What you close for depends on what was agreed upon with the Prospect in the earlier Pre-commitment.

Normally the agreement will be to buy your product. However, in some cases, the action you seek may be an agreement to proceed to another step, such as to cooperate with you in working up a formal cost proposal for a multi-unit order.

To lead up to this request for action, briefly review the objectives agreed-upon earlier. Pause at each objective to gain the Prospect's agreement that your demo satisfied it:

> *"As I showed you a few minutes ago, the GEM 4500 will meet this first objection by _____ . Are we in accord that it did accomplish that objective?"*

When the Prospect nods agreement that each has been accomplished, put another check mark (for completion) beside that item on the flip-chart.

In the same summary manner, work quickly through all of the specified objectives, showing how your product can meet them.

Once you have done that, it's only logical that the Prospect will be ready to sign the order: thus you can proceed on the assumption that the sale has been made, so all that remains is to wrap up the details.

Assuming the sale is acting on the premise that since buying makes such perfect sense the Prospect will naturally agree.

But suppose you find that the Prospect is reluctant to sign the order, even though she agrees that you have indeed proved that each of the objectives settled upon in the earlier Pre-commitment have been accomplished.

By her reluctance to sign, the Prospect is now, by implication, saying that you have not yet proven — to her complete satisfaction — that you can accomplish one or more of the specified objectives.

Deal with that reluctance as an objection, and work through the five-phase process covered in my other books, including **Sales Training Tutorials** www.SalesTrainingSource.com

- **Explore**.

- **Listen through to what is really being said—** don't assume and don't interrupt.

- **Restate**.

- **Respond Positively**; then,

- **Move** On.

Probe to find on precisely what point the Prospect is hung up, and focus on it. Do not let other new issues intrude now; concentrate on the existing objection or hesitation.

Supplement: the "Action Plan" or "Implementation Plan Close"

One of the best ways to close is by using an Action Plan (sometimes termed an Implementation Plan. These detail what you will do for the buyer, and within what time frames.

If the Prospect accepts the Action Plan, then that is in effect agreeing to the purchase.

But what if the Prospect begins discussing or negotiating dates or other details? That is almost certainly a strong buying signal, which indicates that they have "bought" the basic concept and are now fine-tuning the implementation details.

Advantages of using the Action Plan or Implementation Schedule close:

- It assumes the sale.

- It is direct, to the point, and businesslike. The client will respect your professionalism. The schedule shows that you are planning in advance to make sure that the project will be effective.

- Because you have obviously gone to the trouble of planning an implementation schedule, the prospect will be impressed by your interest, and by your confidence.

- If there are any final objections, this will cause them to surface. That way you can deal with them on the spot.

How-to set up for an Action Plan /Implementation Plan Close

If you expect to close with an Action Plan, prepare a visual aid that overviews your proposed installation plan, detailing the steps you will take, as well as the steps to be taken by the client.

- Depending on what kind of visuals you are using, this could be on a flip-chart, A-frame, or projected visual. Or, if the group is very small, on your laptop.

- The model below shows one way of setting up your Implementation/Action Plan.

- Use "real-time" dates specific to this prospect (e.g "June 11"), not generic time-lines like "21 days after signing."

- Go over each item, explaining exactly what it involves. Then present this chart, along with your contract to the prospect, saying, "In order to ensure this completion date I'll need your okay here."

- Caution: be sensitive to the feedback you get. Beware of going into too much detail if the Prospect seems already sold. Bogging down in unneeded detail is one of the most effective way of talking yourself out of a sale.

- Be prepared to negotiate dates and action steps on this plan. Keep in mind that the Prospect's interest in tinkering with the details is a strong signal that he has "bought" the overall plan.

Date	Who is responsible / customer's input	Date
Review of specific requirements	Prospect's name (person who will be signing the contact), plus your name	Today's Date
Your first step	What cooperation you will need from the prospect, such as space, staff help and the like	Add
Your Second step	A contact person with the prospect firm	Add
What other steps you will perform	Ditto	
Wrap up/ conclusion/ Evaluation	Ditto	To be jointly determined

Application Exercise

1. Outline the points you would make in summarizing
    and closing to one of the prospects on the list you
    prepared earlier.

    *   Refer to the objectives and to the specific ways
        in which the product or service you sell will
        achieve each of these objectives.

    *   Rehearse the way in which you would make use
        of any visual aids, samples, the product itself.

2. Prepare an implementation schedule for this
    prospect and rehearse aloud how you would use it
    in closing.

Part three: COMMUNICATING ON MULTIPLE LEVELS

Your overall purpose in giving a demonstration or presentation is, of course, to communicate—that is, to communicate your ideas TO the Prospect, and to comprehend and respond to the communication feedback that comes FROM the Prospect.

We tend to think of communication as primarily a matter of words. But those who study this field find that only around 7% of the messages transmitted during face-to-face communication are carried by the words that are said.

Put differently, 93% of the messages back and forth are conveyed non-verbally, by signals such as facial expressions, eye contact or the lack of it, posture, hand gestures, movements, coming forward to or drawing back from the other person, voice tone, and other subtle mannerisms.

What that tells us is . . .

- first, to be effective in sales, you must be able to use words effectively— that is the verbal part.

- second and perhaps even more important, it's essential to be attuned to the non-verbal messages that are flowing back and forth between salesperson and Prospect.

If, as a salesperson, you're able to read the Prospect's non-verbal signals, you gain extremely valuable insight into what he or she is really thinking.

But, conversely, you also need to be aware not only of what your words are saying, but also of the signals that your voice tone, facial expressions, posture, mannerisms, and the like are sending back to the Prospect.

For example, if you fail to maintain good eye contact, the Prospect may— perhaps subconsciously— feel that you are not trustworthy or not telling the complete truth about your product.

Similarly, if your gestures are too quick and choppy, the Prospect may interpret that as nervousness.

It goes without saying, therefore, that a very important part of your preparation before getting your early demonstrations is to do some dry runs in front of a video camera so that you can see what the Prospect sees.

Section A. Non-verbal techniques for communicating TO Prospects

In communicating to the Prospect during the demo or presentation, two areas are particularly important:

1. The personal image which you project. (Unless your Prospect sees you as professional and reliable, your efforts may be largely wasted.)

2. The way in which you are able to focus the Prospect's attention where it should be.

Let's look at each of these in turn.

1. *Projecting the right image.*

The phrase "projecting an image" has some bad connotations, suggesting doing phony things in order to manipulate people.

We don't mean it that way. Rather, the point is to avoid those small mannerisms and habits that can distract, and hence cause sales presentations and demonstrations to flop.

Presenting a presentation or demonstration can be stressful (particularly when you are new at it), and that stress may bring about unpleasant mannerisms.

The initial nervousness, you may feel at the start could cause you to,

- avoid eye contact.

- have fidgety hands.

- speak too fast and with too much urgency in your voice.

These are the kind of cues that a Prospect could misread into believing that you are a fast-talking, shifty-eyed, high-pressure type, not to be trusted.

> *"An experienced salesperson makes a conscious attempt to impress with slow, wide gestures; a relatively smooth brow; occasional head-on glances; slow, regular, and complete respiratory cycles; a resonant, inflective voice with optimistic timber; a slightly up-tilted chin, and composed hands."*

(This from an old but classic article, "Sign Language Spoken Here," The Marketing Magazine, December 15, 1969.)

Practice, along with regular self-critiques using videotaping will help alleviate the stress and mannerisms that result from inexperience.

Special note: projecting your enthusiasm by your posture and seating position

Way back, Bob Tuomey, then with Xerox Corporation, taught me a subtle tip: a good salesperson sits forward in the chair. That conveys energy and enthusiasm, and in turn may "magnetize" the Prospect to come forward, as well.

You may be tired, but if you want to make the sale, do not make yourself comfortable in that chair.

Synchronicitously, as I was finishing up this e-version of the book, I watched novelist Ken Follett being interviewed on one of the morning programs about his newest book. He sat way forward on the chair, so much so it almost seemed it would roll out beneath him. But his posture conveyed more than his joy at turning a new creation on the world: it somehow subtly brought the viewer into tune: "Hey, he's so charged, so upbeat, this book must really be good! I'll sit forward in my TV chair . . .and then go buy the book!"

2. Focusing the Prospect's attention

The center of attention in a demonstration should be on whatever it is that you are showing — which might be your product, or work samples.

Therefore, if the demonstration is to be effective, it is essential to unclutter your message so the Prospect's attention can focus where it should be. With the extraneous static cleared away, the demonstration can be more effective, and the Prospect more at ease.

In my consulting work, I had the chance to ride along on calls with reps from various organizations. From my notes at that time:

> "The other day I attended a demonstration given by an experienced salesperson, someone I had been told was working below potential. I tried to view it from the Prospect's point of view.

> "The thing that stood out most clearly was the fact that he sat me (as the Prospect) in a chair, then stood in front and lectured like he was a professor and I was his student.

> "But he had set up his A-frame on one side of the machine, and he stood on the other side of it. As a result, I didn't know whether to look at him, or at the machine, or at the A-frame. My eyes kept looking for a spot to focus, and I missed a lot of what he was saying."

Compare that with my observation of a different salesperson in action:

> "Later, I attended another demonstration, this one given by a relatively inexperienced salesperson, but who already ranked number two in the office.

"The difference was amazing. This time, I found my attention focused where it should be all the time, and that made me much more comfortable.

"In fact, he was so good at his job that he was able to move me around the machine — to operate the controls and to do other small tasks — without my realizing what he was doing. His gestures were subtle but clear, and he had me acting as if on subliminal signals."

3. Positioning yourself

The simple matter of where you stand will have a very significant influence on the Prospect and her reactions.

As you know from your own experiences when making sales calls, the desk can be a barrier. Some Prospects deliberately hide behind their desk, using it as a shelter. For others, the desk is a natural obstacle which they try to overcome.

In any case, so long as the desk stands between you and the Prospect, it usually has the psychological effect of putting the two of you on opposite sides.

Much the same operates in the presentation or demonstration. If you spend much of the time facing, "lecturing-at" the Prospect, a psychological barrier may result, and it sets up as "me against him (or her)."

The solution is obvious: whenever possible, stand with— that is, *beside*, not in front of—the Prospect.

If you are demonstrating to a group, try to stand within the group, perhaps walking around, making eye-contact with each member in turn. Overcome any tendency to lecture at the group. By standing with the customer or customers, you convey the message, "we're working together on your problems" — which is in fact what you are doing.

Other tips

Avoid turning your back on the Prospect. This is a matter of courtesy, (not, as you might think, of self-protection)!

Whenever possible stand beside your product or samples. From this position, you can still maintain eye contact and talk to the Prospect, rather than to the wall behind.

Move in a calm, deliberate manner. Never let yourself become rattled or rushed— if you do, the Prospect may interpret this as a sign that your product is confusing or difficult to operate.

4. Moving the Prospect

Depending on what you are demonstrating, it may be best if both you and the Prospect stand during the demonstration. For one thing, she can see your product or samples more in context from a standing position.

Another point: a Prospect who is standing is more likely to become physically involved in your demo, perhaps by touching the product, or viewing samples or performing other small tasks that make him or her at ease with the product.

Sometimes you will need to move the Prospect from one spot to another, perhaps in order to get a better view of the product or work samples.

Even better, accompany that request with movements in which you lead the way by stepping in the direction in which you want the Prospect to move.

You may also accentuate your action with broad, sweeping arm movements. Most people will be instinctively drawn along with the flow of movements.

Sometimes you need the customer to move, but, at the same time, you may not want to interrupt the flow of your demonstration. Or perhaps you have asked the Prospect to move already, and hence may not want to ask again.

In this situation, if you suddenly move backwards, the Prospect will be drawn forward to fill the vacuum you left.

This will be especially effective if you keep talking as you move, and if you then gestured toward some part of your product or samples. (Although this approach may sound almost devious, it works.)

Try experimenting with someone at home or in the office. Or ask them to try it on you sometime when you're not expecting it. You'll find yourself stepping forward without intending to, as if you were drawn in to fill a vacuum.

In few situations, you can acceptably guide the Prospect by a gentle pressure on the arm just above the elbow. But caution: some people are very uncomfortable being touched by strangers.

Application exercise

Sometime soon, when no one else is around (so they don't see you talking to yourself!), set up your video-camera and record some practice sessions as you rehearse what we have covered to this point.

Your objective is two-fold: first, to learn to project smoothness and confidence as you move and speak; second, to self-edit out any distracting mannerisms and speech-patterns.

Here are some items to consider, both in advance, and then later, as you see what worked well and not so well when you watch yourself on the video.

Where you will stand in relation to your product, as well as to the flip-chart, projection screen, or chalk-board. You don't want to be in constant motion, moving from one side to the other. It's usually best if you stand beside the flip-chart or sample, so you can minimize walking back and forth in front of it.

- Where you will be during each part of your demo or presentation. At what points will you be handling the samples or the product, and when will you be writing on the board?

- How you will move unobtrusively from point to point. Your moves should be so smooth that the Prospect is not aware of them, even though she will be listening to what you say as you move.

- If it is a relatively large group, how and when will step into the group, and when will you stand in front? (General rule: start and end in the front and circulate during the presentation.)

- The sense of someone talking from the front tends to bring us back to the old passive teacher-in-front, students-seated mode. That can be okay for a bit. But you can usually make better contact, and bond with the members, if you walk into the center of the group from time to time.

- Again, it's a good idea to visualize the room, and mentally rehearse the points at which you will make these moves.

Also, mentally rehearse how and when you would move the Prospect, using the non-verbal methods above.

Once you are comfortable, try another practice session, again with the video-camera running, though this time with a live person playing the role of the Prospect. Try to get them to view the video with you, sharing their take on how it went.

- Were you clear in the way you said what you did? Did you talk too fast? Too slowly?

- How did you make them feel — as if you and they were working together, or did they feel you were treating them as students?

Section B. Decoding non-verbal cues FROM Prospects

As you conduct the presentation or demonstration, your focus naturally enough will be on what *you* say and do.

But at least equally important are what communications come back to you from the Prospect or others, because that's crucial feedback on when to move on and when to go into more detail.

That means listening with your eyes as well as your ears. Though what people communicate through their gestures and movements is often unconscious on their part, the clues can be invaluable . . . if you know how to read them.

A Prospect with his arms folded across his chest may be telling you, "I'm closed-in and locked up. My arms are my armored vest, and you're not going to get through to me."

How to handle this: if you can cause the arms to open, the mind will (usually) open as well.

- One way is to ask the Prospect to hold something — perhaps samples of your work. It's awkward to hold thing s when your arms are folded.

- Another approach is to ask them to operate the product you are there to demonstrate. A Prospect can't very well keep his arms crossed and push buttons at the same time!

Sometimes a Prospect will find a chair to plop into, even though you've tried to clear them out of the area. Why the chair? Because he may see that chair as a refuge, a secure little island.

To make progress, you need to get the Prospect off that island. Ask him or her to operate the unit you are demonstrating. When you ask them to move, accompany the request with the movement and arm gestures that we discussed on previous pages.

Facial expressions as cues

Glazed eyes and wandering attention usually mean that you have lost the Prospect . . . at least temporarily. Perhaps you're talking about applications which are of no interest to him.

What to do? Speed up the tempo. Or change the subject, or ask questions to bring the Prospect back in.

Or get the Prospect involved by asking a greater number of questions, especially those that require more than a yes or no answer.

You might also spark interest again by asking an *open-ended question*, which encourages the Prospect to talk: "What applications have you seen so far that look particularly useful to you?"

Secret knowledge revealed here for the first time! Many people are usually most involved and interested when they are doing a lot of the talking! *Implication*: Get them talking by asking questions that nudge them to tell what they like about your product.

What do you do if, while you are presenting or demonstrating, the Prospect stares into space, or just looks out the window?

Usually it's best to deal with it directly. Pause your demo, and ask, "I notice there's something about that other machine that attracts your eye. May I ask what it is?"

- The Prospect may realize that his mind was simply wandering, and so will snap back.

- Or, she may give you a clue such as a specific question about the other unit. That may tell you that she really needs a feature on the other unit or may not be as price-sensitive as you had assumed.

Oftentimes, non-verbals need to be read in context. Be alert, then look for other elements to help fill in the picture.

For example, if the Prospect takes his glasses off, it may mean either interest or disbelief. The expression on his face will usually tell you which it is.

However, that mannerism with the eyeglasses may also indicate that he likes what you are saying and is impressed.

But if the Prospect rubs his eyes in the way shown above watch out — it may be a signal that he is not listening.

On the other hand, if the Prospect cups his chin in his hand, or if he rubs his chin, he's probably thinking of ways in which he can use your product.

In that case, it may be wise to slow down your presentation in order to give more thinking time, but don't stop speaking altogether, as silence would break the spell.

But when a Prospect is seated, with his head resting on his hand, he's probably bored and disinterested.

If nothing you say or do seems to light a fire under the Prospect, then try the direct approach: "I notice that I don't seem to be covering the things that are of special interest to you. Can you help me?"

Proximity as a clue

To a very large extent, you can gauge a Prospect's interest by the degree to which he or she comes toward you and the product.

Perhaps you've noticed during sales calls in a Prospect's office that when he leans forward onto the table toward you he is interested and ready to do business. Implication: in a sales call where you are both seated, the object is to "magnetize" and draw him forward.

Similarly, during a presentation or demonstration, when you're both standing, the more the Prospect leans toward you or toward the product you are demonstrating, the more interested he is. Capitalize on this interest.

However, the reverse is also true: if a client draws back physically, she may really be drawing back mentally. If so, your objective should be to "re-magnetize" her. You might do this by stepping slightly toward her to show the details of a work sample or the like.

A caution: most of us draw a mental ring around ourselves, roughly in a 3' to 7' radius. Perhaps unconsciously, we consider this our "private living space," and usually bristle if it is invaded by strangers. (Observe yourself: you may feel uncomfortable, may even draw back, if someone you don't know, or don't like, comes too close.)

When you are giving a demonstration, the Prospect will usually tolerate some invasion of this space, particularly as he grows to trust you. But be careful: if you seem hi grow tense, or begin to back away, then you are probably overstepping. Draw back. When you do that, when you re-open the space, the Prospect will usually relax, and may even come forward toward you.

Spotting buying signals

One category of non-verbal communications deserves special mention: more than a few sales have been lost because the salesperson failed to recognize that the Prospect was ready to buy and was waiting only for the opportunity to sign.

Sometimes a Prospect will tell (or signal) you when he or she is interested, or likes something. Those are clear buying signals.

But often the buying signals are more subtle:

- For example, a Prospect's nodding approval to your major sales points might be indicating a buying signal. If she picks up and re-examines the work samples that you provided, this could also be a buying signal.

- It's usually a promising buying signal if a Prospect asks about practical matters such as cost, payment terms, delivery schedules or similar matters.

Other Prospect remarks that can usually be interpreted as buying signals include questions such as these:

- "Will I need to change my supplies?"

- "Is it difficult to learn how to run this unit?"

- "How soon can it be in place?"

- "Do we need any special insurance to cover this?"

The article I mentioned earlier—decades old, but a classic—traces the typical pattern of the successful sales appeal. ("Sign Language Spoken Here," *The Marketing Magazine*, December 15, 1969) made some excellent additional points.

Note especially the flow of signals as the Prospect opens up and begins transmitting early buying cues.

1. Prospect's eyes are downcast, covered by lives. Face is turned away. Smile is thin lipped, restricted to the mouth, eyes drifting to other things. Translation: you're being shut out.

2. Mouth is relaxed, without the mechanical smile. Ken is forward. Eyes are still averted, but visible. He/she is considering your presentation.

3. Eyes engage yours for several seconds at a time. A slight, one-sided smile, extending at least to nose level. Brows are drawn together. He's weighing your proposal.

4. Head is shifted to the same level as yours. Smile is relaxed, includes mouth, nostrils, and eyes. Eyes are fully visible. Brows are clear or have slight horizontal lines. He's enthusiastic — the sale is virtually made.

Application Exercise

1. Review the examples of the varieties of Prospects' non-verbal signals on the previous pages.

Pause as you look at each block and build your own clear mental picture of a specific person (such as a Prospect to whom you've recently given a demonstration). Picture this person holding the posture, and mentally rehearse how you would react.

For example, picture yourself opening up a "closed-in" Prospect by handing her some samples to hold.

Practice, each of these until you can make the appropriate responses smoothly.

If possible, rehearse them with another person playing the Prospect role.

2. Be alert to the non-verbals and other body-language signals, especially buying cues, which you observe. Note them in a worksheet like this model, along with how you interpret them.

Signal	Typical meaning

Wrap-up application exercise

Before your next presentation or demonstration, review the exercises you've worked through in this book, pulling them together into a unified whole that is comfortable to you, and consistent with your personal style and manner.

Rehearse the demo by yourself, preferably in front of a mirror or, even better, a video camera so that you can review the results.

Use the demonstration preplanning checklist below is a tool in organizing yourself. And other items to it that are appropriate to your own product or situation.

Demonstration/ presentation pre-planning checklist

Settle the location and reserve a room, if necessary.

Check your product to be sure. It is working correctly. If it needs special plugs or outlets make sure that you have them available.

Check any work samples that you are bringing to make sure that they are complete.

Prepare any PowerPoint slides, handouts, or other materials.

Arrange everything in the order in which it will be used.

Confirm with the Prospect that the timing is still suitable. Do this either the afternoon before or the morning of the presentation.

Make sure the Prospect has clear directions to where you will be meeting.

Rehearse and fully prepare each use that you plan to present to the Prospect.

If the meeting is to be held on your premises, be sure to welcome the attendees as they arrive. They are new turf, so do what you can to make them comfortable as guests.

Other books in my two series:

- **The Small Business Sales How-to Series, and,**
- **Career Savvy People Skills Series**

The books in the two series described here flow from my experience first as a lawyer, then a management consultant working with companies that included Xerox in the United States, Canada and Europe; Kodak; Sylvania; Bank of America; Motorola, and others.

Part of my work involved analyzing the key skills and competencies that make the difference between top-performing managers, sales people and sales managers, then developing training programs, guides, and job-aids to teach these skills to new trainees and those who had been working below their full potential. The books in this series draw from that experience.

See my blog/website at **www.Selling-face-to-face.com** for additional tips and ideas, as well as contributions by other readers.

I hope that *How to Deliver Professional Sales Presentations & Demonstrations* has been helpful to you. If so, then as a favor I'd appreciate your leaving a reader review on the Amazon page. Here's the link directly to the page:

https://www.amazon.com/review/create-review?&asin=B07NVTC55T

The illustrations of non-verbals were borrowed (with consent) from sales guides I developed for various divisions of Xerox.

Thank you,

Michael

Books in the *SMALL BUSINESS SALES HOW-TO SERIES:*

Book #1: 25 SALES HOW-TO TUTORIALS

Small Business Sales How-to
Book #1

25 Sales How-to Tutorials

A Step-by-step Guide for New Entrepreneurs, Self-employed, Career Changers

Michael McGaulley

TUTORIALS is a step-by-step guide for new entrepreneurs, self-employed folks, and career changers. It's built tutorials that you don't just read but go beyond and use as models for developing your own sales messages. It's especially targeted to the needs of career-changers and people going off on their own, or looking for a new job or a new field—such as consultants, free-agents, or independent contractors.

Book #2: SELLING 101: CONSULTATIVE SELLING SKILLS

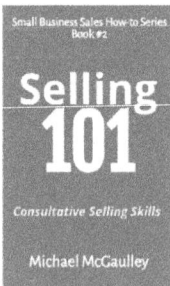

Small Business Sales How-to Series
Book #2

Selling 101

Consultative Selling Skills

Michael McGaulley

SELLING 101 is directed to more experienced salespeople who want access the kind of sales training courses I developed for major marketing firms including Xerox, Kodak, and others.

Book #3: SALES TRAINING WORKSHOP LEADER GUIDE

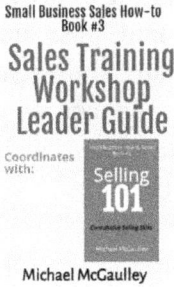

THE *SALES TRAINING WORKSHOP LEADER GUIDE* is the instructor's guide coordinated with the text, *Selling 101: Consultative Selling Skills.*

Who this sales training workshop-- leader guide is intended for

Sales managers looking for materials for sales team meetings.

Instructors in new entrepreneur training workshops.

Instructors in community colleges or similar job-training programs

What this sales training workshop - leader guide provides

The 14 Modules in the Workshop Leader Guide track the coverage in *SELLING 101*, linking to specific pages for ease in linking across.

A chart at the start of each Module provides a succinct overview of what that module is about, suggested time to allow, as well as materials and set-up.

The content within the modules guide the instructor or leader through clearly-marked sections, such as

- Overview and set context,
- Lead discussion,
- Explain,
- Pair trainees for one-on-one role plays,

- Conduct whole-group debriefing, and,
- Wrap-up and overview the next module.

Pre-class assignments for each module are provided, which the workshop leader can copy and pass out in advance. These guide the trainee on the reading assignment (chapters or sections from the course text, Selling 101), as well as other preparation, such as discussions and role-play exercises to prepare for.

Book #4:   HOW TO DELIVER PROFESSIONAL PRESENTATIONS   & DEMONSTRATIONS

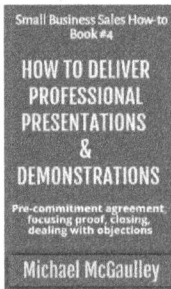

Small Business Sales How-to
Book #4

HOW TO DELIVER
PROFESSIONAL
PRESENTATIONS
&
DEMONSTRATIONS

Pre-commitment agreement,
focusing proof, closing,
dealing with objections

Michael McGaulley

HOW TO DELIVER PROFESSIONAL PRESENTATIONS   & DEMONSTRATIONS covers the practical how-to of presenting or demonstrating in front of the prospect, as well as the very important matter of reading (and sending) non-verbal messages.   It also addresses the essential point that demonstrations, presentations, proposals, free-trials, discounts and other special deals are "proof sources," given for a specific, defined purpose, agreed-upon in advance with the prospective buyer.

Books in the *CAREER SAVVY PEOPLE SKILLS SERIES:*

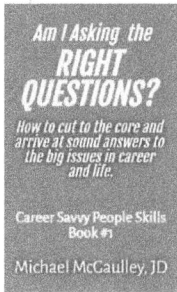

Book #1: *AM I ASKING THE RIGHT QUESTIONS?*

Am I Asking the
RIGHT QUESTIONS?
How to cut to the core and arrive at sound answers to the big issues in career and life.

Career Savvy People Skills
Book #1

Michael McGaulley, JD

"You've got to stay aware of the games that are being played. You don't have to play the games yourself, but you do need to recognize when they are being played against you."

RIGHT QUESTIONS *provides an array of tools for cutting* to cut to the core and arriving at sound answers to the big issues in career and life.

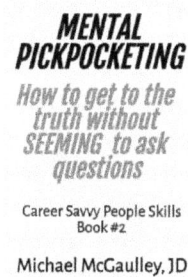

Book #2: MENTAL PICKPOCKETING

MENTAL PICKPOCKETING
How to get to the truth without SEEMING to ask questions

Career Savvy People Skills
Book #2

Michael McGaulley, JD

When you ask a question, most people, most of the time, will do their best to tell the truth. But not always.

MENTAL PICKPOCKETING introduces you to an array of methods for getting to the truth without *seeming* to ask questions.

Book #3: UN-PUZZLING PERSONALITIES

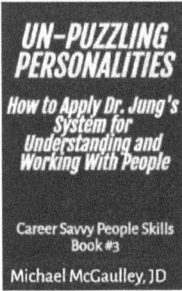

UN-PUZZING PERSONALITIES is based on a system developed by Carl Jung for understanding and working with individuals, teams, and other groups.

Use it for viewing yourself from fresh perspective, as well as a tool for understanding the different ways others perceive and react to events and communications.

Websites:

SalesTrainingSource.com

MichaelMcGaulley.net

Legal and copyright notices continued from the front of this book

Necessary legal disclaimers, provisos, and such

The contents of this book reflect the author's views acquired through experience in the areas addressed. The author is not engaged in rendering any legal, financial or accounting advice. Business customs, courtesies, and legal implications vary with the context, and with geographic region or country. Accordingly, anyone reading this material should not rely totally on the contents herein, and should seek the advice of others. The author has made his best effort to ensure that this is a helpful and informative manual. The contents are recommendations only, and the author cannot take responsibility for loss or action to any individual or corporation acting, or not acting, as a result of the material presented here.

While the information contained within the pages of this electronic book, other related books and e-books, and the related web-site, is periodically updated, no guarantee is given that the information provided is correct, complete, and/or up-to-date.

The materials contained in this e-book and related website are provided for general information purposes only and do not constitute legal or other professional advice on any subject matter. Neither the author nor publisher accept any responsibility for any loss which may arise from reliance on information contained in this book or related website.

Some links within this e-book or related website may lead to other websites, including those operated and maintained by third parties. The author and publisher of this e-book include these links solely as a convenience to you, and the presence of such a link does not imply a responsibility for the linked site or an endorsement of the linked site, its operator, or its contents.

The publisher and author accept no liability whatsoever for any losses or damages caused or alleged to be caused, directly or indirectly, by utilization of any information contained herein, or obtained from any of the persons or entities herein above.

This book and related website and its contents are provided "AS IS" without warranty of any kind, either express or implied, including, but not limited to, the implied warranties of merchantability, fitness for a particular purpose, or non-infringement.

If you, or any other reader, do not agree to these policies as noted above, please do not use these materials or any services offered herein.

Your use of these materials indicates acceptance of these policies.

The illustrations of non-verbals were borrowed (with consent) from sales guides I developed for various divisions of Xerox.

Part of my work involved analyzing the key skills and competencies that make the difference between top-performing managers, salesperson and sales managers, then developing training programs, guides, and job-aids to teach these skills to new trainees and those who had been working below their full potential. The books in this series draw from that experience.

See my blog and website at www.SalesTrainingSource.com for additional tips and ideas, as well as contributions by other readers.

www.ingramcontent.com/pod-product-compliance
Lightning Source LLC
Chambersburg PA
CBHW060634210326
41520CB00010B/1606